Idea Magic

How to Generate Innovative Ideas and Put Them into Action

By Michael Sloan

Table of Contents

Introduction:

Creation! There is nothing more powerful to the human spirit than the art of creating something incredible! We as humans have a tremendous ability to use our imaginations to create incredible ideas. With the power of imagination skyscrapers have been built, world wonders have been engineered, beautiful movies have been created and gorgeous paintings have captured our imaginations. Yet there can be a time when we are feeling a little low on the imagination tank, we might feel our ideas aren't coming as quickly as we once hoped or worse, we might feel that we are entirely out of ideas! What are we to do when the ideas aren't coming as quickly as we want? Should we give up? No! Instead of growing frustrated when you can't seem to get the idea machine running, we have a different proposal for you! Within this book you will discover a new way of thinking when it comes to generating ideas, we're going to show you how you can create new and interesting ideas easily and quickly!

With Idea Magic, you can break through the creative constraints that are holding you back from achieving your dreams and unleash the creative beast that is within! We're going to cover the philosophy of what it means to be creative and innovative, discuss the things that happen in our everyday life that destroys innovation and then finally talk about how to generate innovative ideas with ease! If you've always been looking for ways to overcome the creative blocks that stop you from coming up with smart and clever ideas, then read on!

Chapter 1: The Nature of Inspiration

As we begin on our quest for great ideas and innovation, we must first consider what the nature of inspiration actually is. We must understand where it comes from and we must understand how it interacts with us. Quite simply put, inspiration is the process of receiving an influx of creative energy that allows for you to think of interesting and new ideas. Inspiration is the backbone of creativity, for it is where we get our sense of excitement and readiness for action. An artist without inspiration is an artist who will not have the necessary creativity to achieve her dreams. A businessman who has no inspiration will not look at his business with a creative lens and might never be able to fulfill his full potential as a leader. We need inspiration in order to function as creative individuals.

So, if we are dependent on inspiration in order to get things done in a creative manner, where does inspiration come from? There is often an idea that inspiration is a kind of mythical creature, like a unicorn that is hidden away from us and we must search after it diligently. If we make too much noise, this unicorn will run far from us and we will be unable to have our inspiration. Some people think that the best way to get inspiration is to sit around and wait for it to arrive. They hope that this mythical unicorn will visit them and until they receive a visit from their inspiration, they don't' get anything done. Yet that leaves us in a predicament if we were to act that way because it leaves us dependent on some outside force to assist us in our work. This viewpoint, that inspiration is some external force leaves us in a state of helplessness, dependent on the whims of something that we cannot control.

Believe it or not, but the external view of inspiration is one of the most popular views there is. Many people like to think of the artist sitting back and waiting patiently for just the right moment or mood to strike. Many like to imagine that inspiration comes in the middle of the night to the poet, the artist or the creative individual, usually in some kind of fantastical manner, such as a dream striking them or them having a powerful vision of what the future is. This idea of inspiration stems primarily from a romanticized look at the creative process. No one sees the artist working for hours upon hours on his project, constantly revising and changing the way his work looks. No one sees the discarded first, second and third draft of the author, they just see the end result.

When the process of inspiration is ignored, the idea of someone suddenly being struck by a big and bold idea seems as if it were some kind of magic. But that view of inspiration cuts our own ability to generate inspiration out completely. This external view is an extremely popular one, but it has one major underlying assumption. That assumption is that we can do nothing to control or produce inspiration, rather we are at the mercy of some kind of external force that arrives whenever it feels like. So, what are these fatal assumptions? Let's list them out.

Inspiration Assumption One: Only Certain People Can Have It

We often hear the phrase "oh I could never be creative," or "that man's so much more talented than I'll ever be." Many times, there is an underlying assumption about creativity or ingenuity that creates this false idea that it is inherent to a specific person. This belief usually stems from the idea that the external force of inspiration is somehow more available to those creative individuals. Instead of looking to refine and grow in their own sense of creativity, a person could easily and quickly chalk it up to being some kind of innate talent that the creative person has no control over either. This leads an individual to assuming they aren't really capable of being creative or inspired and so they never bother to look any deeper within themselves.

Yet if we were to look at those who are very creative, those who have big ideas, we can actually look at a trend and pattern within them. They often spend long hours working on projects. They are usually quite loose and honest with their work, they have a sense of curiosity and discovery within them. They aren't afraid of failure. If you looked at every creative individual you know, you might notice that they seem to be struck by inspiration often, but that's because they are often in places where they are able to find inspiration. An artist is no different than any other person, it's just they are usually working towards their goal of doing creative work and in the process, they become more creative.

Inspiration Assumption Two: Creativity just happens

The idea of an individual shouting "Eureka!" as they suddenly have a brilliant idea is deeply imbedded in the modern-day perception of the creative. We often look at moments of inspiration as being solitary events and that creates more of a mystery around the idea of being creative. An idea that suddenly arrives uninvited cannot be contained or forced. That perception of creativity being a lightning bolt that strikes a person makes even the idea of developing a creative mindset to be unobtainable. How can we develop creativity if it were a natural event that happens somewhat at random?

The reality is that the lightning bolt of creativity isn't actually a single event at all. Rather it is a process that takes quite a bit of time. The creative process leads up to that single moment of "aha!" but it takes time, effort and focus to be able to reach that point. Consider how Thomas Edison invented the lightbulb. He didn't wake up one morning after having some kind of crazy dream that told him how to figure out how to create a lightbulb, rather he spent countless amounts of hours on experimentation.

The process eventually led to the "aha!" moment where he was able to figure out how to make the lightbulb work.

We see this all across history. Whenever there is some famous figure who discovered something quite brilliant there is a lot of work behind it. Inspiration at the end of the day comes from a place of continuous effort. If you continue to work to be more creative, you will eventually find inspiration. One classic myth about Isaac Newton was the way he discovered gravity. The usual story is that he was sitting underneath a tree when suddenly an apple fell on his head, causing him to realize gravity existed. Of course, things were always falling in Newton's world, so was that really the first time he had witnessed something fall down? Not at all! The real story is that he was pondering how gravity worked to begin with and once he saw the apple fall down, he began to seriously consider why they always fell perpendicular to the ground. His mind had already been forming ideas, the impetus (seeing the apple) just caused his imagination to spark. And that little spark helped ignite all of the ideas that he already had in his head.

Inspiration Assumption Three: Inspiration is a feeling

One of the most dangerous assumptions that you can have in the creative world is to believe that you must be in a specific kind of mood to be creative. If you are looking to create some big idea but you aren't feeling that inspired, you might put off your work until you feel like it later. This is a dangerous assumption because it is based off of something that cannot be controlled. We cannot control our moods and emotions. We don't really have the ability to summon an emotion or a mood on command and so if you find yourself in desperate need for ideas but you aren't in the right mood, you might be in trouble.

Yet the idea that inspiration is based on feelings or moods is erroneous. Inspiration doesn't come from an emotional place, because once again that turns inspiration into a single external force that we are unable to control. Inspiration comes from long hours of hard work and cultivation. If we wait for a proper mood to strike us in order to get creative work done, we'll never get our work done. Imagine if a famous and prolific writer were to wait until he felt like writing, when would his work ever be completed? The truth is that most productive and creative work is done regardless of the mood of the individual. If you wait until you are inspired to write, you will be in trouble. Yet if you write until you feel inspired, you will experience something entirely different. You will find that you aren't required to be held hostage by your feelings, instead you have the ability to get more work done as well as develop a greater sense of creativity.

So, we've talked about some fatal assumptions when it comes to creating inspiration in your life. We've seen that inspiration isn't an external event that arrives on its own and then leaves without permission from the creative. So, where does inspiration actually come from then? It comes from within the individual! The nature of inspiration is that it is an internal process, not an external event. A process happens over time; it doesn't happen instantly. So, what do I mean when I say that inspiration is a process? Well, let's look at it like this: instead of inspiration being some kind of mythical creature that you have to chase down, imagine that it is instead a plant. Everyone has different types of plants and everyone has different sized plants, but we all have access to the same tools to nourish that plant. The attention that we pay to our own inspiration and creativity levels will determine how creative we are in the long run.

This is great news! This means that you have the ability to become just as creative as a brilliant artist, you can generate ideas like da Vinci and you have all of the tools necessary to become the next Steve Jobs in terms of innovation and industry! But having tools at your disposal isn't all that's necessary to create brilliant ideas, you've got to learn what those tools are and how to use them. We talked about how inspiration is more like a plant than a unicorn, so what are the tools that we need to use to nourish and grow that plant of inspiration? Let's move onto the next chapter to find out!

Chapter 2: The Tools of Inspiration

So now that we've established that inspiration doesn't happen in a single, isolated event, we must now begin to consider the implication. The implication is that we are able to grow and develop our own inspiration. So how do we create the mindset that will allow for us to be more creative in our lives? If the tools for inspiration are within us, how can we access them?

Well the first step is to start looking at inspiration as something that you already have access to. You are no different than any other person on the planet, including those of whom we would consider to be really successful and brilliant people. Society and history both like to look at the famous and skilled creative as special and unique and oftentimes we can get caught up in looking at somebody else's life with a feeling that we will never be like them. The truth of the matter is that even though we are all unique and different, we are all made up of the same stuff. We have different temperaments and personalities, but we are united by the fact that we are all human. No one is out of reach; everything can be learned. You must embrace that you can become a creative individual and that you can create innovative ideas with ease.

Once you've made the conscious decision to start looking at yourself as creative, you then have a chance to learn all of the tips and tricks that foster inspiration. So, let's go ahead and look at all of the different tools we have in our inspiration arsenal.

Inspiration Tool One: Curiosity

One of the greatest tools in the arsenal of creating innovative ideas is the question why. The word why is often used as a way to poke and prod and assist in learning information about the world around you. When a child is very young, he begins to ask the question why and usually tries to understand everything in the world around him. He gets into the habit of being curious about the world and until that curiosity becomes punished by adults, he will remain interested and inquisitive. Yet something happens along the way for the curious child. He reaches a point where his parents find it annoying that he asks why all the time. He might be refused answers as he grows up and soon the question of why is quickly answered with "because I said so."

Curiosity diminishes once we hit the schooling industry as well. As our education system takes us in, we are quickly taught a lot of things and the information is served to us. We stop developing a need to search for answers because the teacher's job is to provide them to us. So, our curiosity wanes. Soon we start finding more and more answers and eventually cynicism sets in. The cynical perspective of the teen years replaces the question of why with a rebellious attitude. Curiosity becomes rejection and in the process, the teenager begins to rebel against their parents. They question openly what their parents believe and their parents often punish them for questioning them. This leads to a paradoxical situation where the child begins to feel pressure to fall in line and stop asking questions. In adult life, the wrong question at the wrong time, regardless of how innocent it may be, can be career ending. So, we learn to opt for safety instead of curiosity. Our natural inquisitiveness wanes the more we learn about the world and as such, we lose a crucial piece of our ability to become inspired.

The question of why forces us to look at basic assumptions. Curiosity allows you to ask questions freely and without judgment. For example, look at Henry Ford, the creator of the model T. He was curious enough to ask why we had to transport ourselves with horses. He asked if there was a better way to do it. When the assembly line was developed, it started with a question of why. Why was it that we needed to build things one at a time? The developer of the assembly line figured out a brilliant idea but it started with a question. Why do we do it this way? These questions spark curiosity and the process of learning to answer those questions will lead to a greater chance of discovery.

It's in this process of discovering the answer to a question that allows for inspiration to grow. When you constantly question why things are the way they are, you are allowing your mind space to consider underlying premises that might be false. When a false premise is discovered, when you find out that there is something that could be done better, that is when inspiration begins to grow.

If you want to be in a constant state of figuring out new and better things, if you want to come up with brilliant ideas then you need to be in a state of constant curiosity. Henry Ford once said "If I asked people what they wanted, they would have asked for faster horses." This attitude, the "faster horses" attitude is prevalent within our world. People don't look to expand their imaginations, they aren't curious enough to see what works or ask why things are the way they are and as a result, their curiosity diminishes. They don't find inspiration and they aren't inspired because they have nothing to be inspired about.

Inspiration Tool Two: Purpose

The key to finding innovation and inspiration is being able to find a sufficient reason to be inspired. This might seem redundant but think about it for a minute. As the phrase goes, necessity is the mother of invention. If you want to be inspired, then you must have something in your life that is requiring that inspiration. A great artist or inventor doesn't create simply because they feel they are required to. Some of the greatest creations in the world, some of the greatest achievements in mankind happened not because someone felt obligated to but rather because they derived a greater sense of purpose from it.

Consider the Wright Brothers. They had no funding, no formal education and no crowd of people surrounding them as they worked on their great scheme. The plan? It was to build a flying machine and their heart's greatest desire was to see it come to fruition. This sense of purpose invigorated them and challenged them on a constant basis, forcing them to continually seek out inspiration on how to develop innovative ideas.

If we want to have a developed sense of inspiration, if we want to develop great ideas, we must have some sense of necessity and purpose. We must have a passion that lies deep within our hearts. If we don't have this sense of passion and purpose, then we run the risk of simply looking at our efforts with a lukewarm reception. A lack of passion will destroy any attempts to become inspired because when you aren't passionate, you have no real purpose in your work. Without purpose, we lose the impetus to continually improve. That pressure to improve, the desire to get better and achieve one's purpose is what contributes actively to developing more inspiration. Think of it like this, the greater sense of purpose and desire that you have, the harder you are going to work to achieve your goals. Creativity and innovation is spurred on by having a refined sense of caring about what you're doing, so if you aren't in a place where you have a sense of purpose, then you most likely won't have creativity.

This is particularly why it's so hard for us to inspire such creativity in the corporate work field. Most people aren't really happy with their jobs and don't feel like there's any purpose in it and without that feeling of purpose, our creativity diminishes. That's why a lot of successful companies work extremely hard to imbue their workers with a sense of purpose, so that the worker is able to become more innovative.

So, if you are finding that you aren't particularly creative in a field, or if you are having trouble coming up with ideas, ask yourself if you really feel like you have a purpose in what you are doing. If you're in a place where you aren't feeling particularly inspired because you see the work as menial or meaningless, you're most likely not going to gain inspiration until you learn to change your perspective. Sometimes it's just a matter of learning how to expand the way you think.

Inspiration Tool Three: Perspective

There were once two men laying bricks on the side of the road. When asked what, they were doing one man said "I'm laying bricks," and the other man said "I'm building a hospital." They were doing the exact same thing, but they had very different perspectives. Those perspectives changed the way the men work. One man is willing to work extremely hard because he has a perspective that he is doing something incredible, yet the other man might work hard but won't be as inspired and motivated as the one who sees the end goal. If you want to develop a strong sense of creativity and innovation, you're going to need to be able to develop the perspective to look at what you are doing with a higher level of thinking.

We call this thinking "high altitude thinking." Imagine how things look like when you zoom out and look at everything in play. Consider how a football game looks from the perspective of a player versus someone in the stands. A player can only see what's in front of him, so his ability to come up with plans is limited to his perspective. He can only see what's to his right and left, not what's behind him, not what's way ahead of him. Yet someone who is in the stands can see the entire game. He has a higher perspective and as such this allows for him to formulate strategies about the whole picture. This is why football teams often have individuals able to watch the entire game from a higher perspective and give advice as to what he's seeing.

Do we have this kind of mindset when it comes to considering problems? Oftentimes we can get so caught up with what's in front of us that we don't really think about the big picture. Yet perspective is what allows us to develop that big picture mindset. The effort to take a step back and look at all of the moving parts when searching for a solution will improve your creativity significantly. If you want to have unlimited innovation, then you need to learn how to break through your limited perspective. If our perspectives are limited, then we won't be able to come up with groundbreaking ideas and have unfettered creativity. Perspective can make or break an individual.

So, what does it mean to have to push past your perspective limitations? Well, it starts with thinking about how a problem looks like from a different angle. For example, if you are trying to figure out how to decrease your shipping costs of a product for your company, you might become very focused on how to reduce the cost of the shipping by finding the best possible price. So, you shop around, search, look around but can never really find the thing that you want because it just doesn't exist. A way to develop a better perspective on the situation is to look around and think about the big picture. The point isn't to get a lower priced shipping company, it's to get a lower shipping cost, so maybe you need to change the material so it's cheaper. Perhaps you need to figure out how to move your distribution center to where it would be easier to ship from.

Perspective protects us from our natural inclination to become extremely focused on one single detail. You often hear the phrase "he can only see the trees, not the forest." That perspective of looking only at the thing in front of you will limit your ability to see the whole picture. Learning to take a step back and consider everything, to look at all of the moving parts and ask yourself a series of questions about assumptions will enable you to get a better perspective on everything around you. The more you are willing to stop focusing on just one thing and try to reframe your problem the greater chance you will have of a breakthrough.

There are plenty of great ways to reframe a problem. For example, you could sit down and write out what's going on and list all of the solutions. Then try to think of solutions that aren't on your list. You could bounce your ideas off of a friend who is willing to challenge your assumptions and provide you with perspective. You could even stop what you are doing and try to do something entirely different for a short time, then come back and look at it with fresh eyes. Part of learning new perspective is changing things up so that you aren't sticking around with your regular patterns of thought. The normal human pattern of thought is to become too focused on what it already knows, the goal is to learn something that you don't know. So, you need to be in a continuous state of changing your perspective. This will build up your inspiration and creativity over time like you wouldn't believe!

Inspiration Tool Four: Obsession

If you want to be inspired about something, then you need to be obsessed with it. If you look at all of the famous people in the world who have a seemingly endless supply of ideas, innovation and creativity, most likely they are also people who have a great sense of obsession with what they are doing. Obsession goes past an interest. We often joke about something being an obsession, looking at someone who enjoys a specific hobby and calling that an obsession, but what does it mean to be obsessed?

True and healthy obsession is one where you are unable to stop thinking, reading, learning and talking about a subject. It is within this obsession where you will find the greatest sparks of creativity. The more you learn, the more you digest, the more you understand the topic at hand, the more possibilities that will come to mind. If you are someone who hasn't fully committed himself to learning everything that you can about a field, if you aren't interested in getting as much information as possible about the subject that you want to generate ideas in, then you are seriously limiting your opportunity to be creative.

The more you think, talk and obsess over something, the greater chance you will have of finding inspiration. A good designer isn't creative because he was born that way, he is creative because he can't stop thinking about the design process. Brilliant performers and athletes are the way they are because they train with an obsessive nature. We are often warned about not being too obsessed with things, we are warned to have a balance in our lives. But if we're looking to become successful and achieve our dreams through innovation then we are going to have to come to terms with the fact that an ordinary amount of interest in something will not produce extraordinary results. We must become obsessed with what we are doing. Read as much as you can, talk about it with other likeminded people, look for ways to constantly be thinking, planning and studying. The more you do to think about your work, the more your mind will develop a habit of thinking about your project. That will transfer into your unconscious mind and over time you will find that you will quickly and easily find inspiration and innovation about the subject matter.

Think about obsession like water. The more water you give your mind, the more room you have to swim around. If you don't have a lot of water in your pool, you can't really swim anywhere. But if the pool is completely flooded and full of water, you can swim around just fine. Obsession must fill your mind at all times, it must overtake you so that you are in a constant state of "swimming." This will allow you to develop a greater sense of inspiration over time.

Inspiration Tool Five: Competition

We as humans tend to be very competitive creatures. This can help stimulate our mind and give us a sense of excitement when we work toward a goal. And competition can also force innovation. When Henry Ford invented the Model T he wasn't really interested in changing the color of it from anything except black. He didn't care about what the people wanted and he stuck to what he was comfortable with. Yet what happened once other companies started making their own cars with different colors? It forced Henry Ford to release a new model T with a different color. All throughout history you can see how competition has fundamentally improved or changed a product. Look at the battle between Apple and Microsoft. Both of them can't afford to get lazy because if they do, their rivals will overtake them. This forces them to be in a constant state of innovation. This is good, creative pressure that allows for someone to move past their own complacency.

So, if you want to develop a greater sense of inspiration and become more innovative then you might want to consider adding some competitive aspect to your life. Perhaps if you made a friendly wager with a friend, or challenged someone to a competition of sorts, you might find a greater level of excitement and energy. Nothing can stimulate a person more than a good, healthy sense of competition. If you are in an actual field where you need to be competitive, then you might want to consider learning enough about your competition to teach you how to do things better than them. This will improve your ability to gain perspective as well as give you an edge over your competition.

Sometimes we might discount competition because it feels like it's not very nice to compete. Yet it is this sense of competition that will allow for us to achieve the very best things. Just because you are competing with someone doesn't mean you have to hate them, fight with them or feel negatively towards them. It just means that you are striving to excel past them. They will strive to get past you as well. It's just human nature, so you might want to take advantage of it!

Inspiration Tool Six: Momentum

Sometimes one of the greatest tools in the inspiration arsenal can simply be momentum. There can be many instances of a person waiting for lightning to hit them, they can't wait to experience some greater degree of attention from the unicorn of inspiration, but it never comes. So, they shuffle around and hopelessly wait for something that will never arrive. Don't be like that! Instead try considering the fact that inspiration develops greatly in those who have the greatest amount of momentum in their lives! What do I mean by momentum? I mean the act of moving forward as you work, even if you aren't feeling particularly inspired.

Inspiration and innovation happen over time. The more you work, the greater chance you have of allowing your momentum to carry you into an inspired moment. Instead of waiting for something that will never come, choose to work toward your goal and be diligent in your efforts. It might take a long time, it might take longer than you want, but eventually you will reach a point of inspiration. You will have that great idea; you will be excited and full of creativity. But if you aren't constantly working toward that goal, if you aren't trying to come up with new ideas every day, then realistically there won't be much of a chance for you to receive that kind of inspiration. You've got to be constantly working toward your goals in order to be in a place where such inspiration will arrive.

This means you can't rely on your feelings or moods to get you to work. You've got to make a commitment to work every single day, even if you aren't feeling it. Stephen King believes that writing consistently is more important than writing when you feel inspired because when you wait until you are inspired, you won't ever reach your goals. If your mood only comes once a week then you have six days of waiting around. But if you work six days and on the seventh day you have that brilliant idea, you still have six days of work behind you. It's really that simple! So, don't wait for a mood, don't hope to have lightning strike you, instead build up momentum by working every single day. You'll find that the more consistently you work, the more ideas and innovation you will have.

Inspirational Tool Seven: Inspirational People

If you want to become more inspired in your life, if you want to cultivate a greater sense of excitement so that you can unleash your inner creativity, then you might want to consider looking for inspirational people. There is no shortage of great motivational speakers in the world. You don't have to look really hard to find great podcasts about inspiration and motivation. There are thousands of books dedicated to the subject. If you aren't using these tools, then you are giving up a very essential resource.

A lot of times you'll see the same situation: someone listens to an inspirational speaker, they get all fired up and then come Monday, nothing happens. They fizzle out. You might see someone as an inspiration junkie, running from speaker to speaker, from book to book, method to method, but never really changing their lives. We don't want to be like that, we don't want to derive our entire source of inspiration from external things, rather we want to supplement our lives with those sources of inspiration. Supplementation helps out but isn't the main source of our nutrition. Remember, we want to cultivate a plant here, we want to help our inspiration and innovation grow, so we want to pour plenty of water on it. So, don't look at inspirational speakers as the main source of your inspiration, rather look at them as a tool to help motivate you.

It's good to be in a constant state of consumption about the things that inspire you directly. A steady diet of podcasts, speakers, blog posts and books will keep you moving, even when you feel like your inspiration is incredibly low. Sometimes they will provide you with the perfect boost that will help you break through a wall. We all get there sometimes, there are some days when it's really hard to push yourself, so surrounding yourself with resources that will help your motivation level increase will be of the utmost importance.

Another excellent source of inspiration is other people. If you find someone who is likeminded, or interested in the same things that you are interested in, if you're in the company of a group of people who are all inspiring, then you yourself will be able to benefit from that. There is tremendous value in associating and aligning yourself with people who inspire you. These people will assist you in achieving great things and in kind you are able to assist them as well. When two people are together, they have a great chance of pushing one another forward than if they were alone.

We as humans are social creatures and so when we begin to work with another person or group, we might find that as long as the group is a healthy and friendly one, our creativity and innovation might skyrocket. This is an excellent thing because it allows for us to overcome our natural limitations and perspectives. No two people are alike and so they are able to challenge and push one another to greatness. This is an incredible thing to experience and it ultimately can create the perfect environment for innovation. If you look at history, there are a great number of people who had brilliant partners and co-workers who assisted them in their plans. When you have a partner in crime you are increasing your ability twofold. This will serve you well in your plans to create innovative ideas!

So, those are some exceptional tools meant to help you develop a sense of creativity in your life. If you want to grow in your inspiration and learn how to think outside of the box, these are ways of thinking that will ultimately help refine that sense of inspiration in you. Remember, inspiration must come from within and it is a process, not a solitary event. So, if the act of gaining great ideas doesn't happen instantaneously and is instead a process, what else is there to consider? Well, we've talked a great deal about all of the good things that will help nourish your creativity and inspiration, but that's only half of the picture. When you assist a plant in growing, you don't just pour water on it and leave it in the sun. You also make sure to remove the dead branches and keep pests away from killing it. If we want strong, healthy inspiration levels then we must be willing to look at some of the potential things that harm our inspiration. Let's move onto the next chapter and look at some of the things that kill our inspiration.

Chapter 3: Inspiration Killers

Inspiration must be grown within, but there are weeds that can rise up and strangle our inspiration. They will choke and murder our creativity and before we can even get started on our ideas and dreams, we might feel a loss of inspiration. So, in order to develop a greater sense of inspiration and creativity, we must be willing to look at some of the things that damage our inspiration. These things, believe it or not, always come from within. We might have external things that happen to us, but at the end of the day, we are the ones who choose whether we are going to allow them to affect us. So, let's go ahead and get started looking at the many inspiration killers.

Inspiration Killer One: Lack of Confidence

Have you ever had a great idea but then immediately realized that it was impossible? Have you ever been in a situation where other people have sabotaged themselves because they refuse to believe that they are capable of actually carrying an idea out? This all stems from a lack of confidence in yourself.

If you are confident then you are giving yourself permission to have as many ideas as you like. When they arrive and they seem doable, your confidence is what allows them to come into existence. For example, if you have an idea about how to save money on your cable bill, if you were confident you would pick up the phone and call the cable company immediately to handle it. Yet if there was a lack of confidence, you might try to convince yourself it won't work, without even trying it! Then over time, as you live a life without any confidence, you might find that your ideas aren't coming to mind as readily or easily anymore. Why? Because you kill them out of the gate with your lack of confidence! The less confident that you are, the less of a chance that you will have a great idea. Instead you will *think* that any idea that you have won't work. This is a perspective problem entirely.

A confident person can reasonably and accurately judge his ideas on their merits. He might decide against a course of action based on what he knows to be true, but it's not coming from a lack of confidence. Rather it's coming from a place of security in knowing that the idea itself is objectively good or bad. But someone who has no confidence doesn't really have the ability to judge between good or bad because they don't feel confident in themselves, so they judge everything they think of as bad. Then as their lives continue, they find themselves in an emotional hole where they can't really seem to think of any good ideas. Then they blame themselves for their inability to be innovative and their confidence continues to decrease.

This brutal cycle is a reality in many people's lives. There are a great many who have been told that their ideas are bad and because of it they begin to feel like they can't do anything right. So, they stop trying on a subconscious level. Consciously they are still working hard to come up with ideas, but the deepest part of themselves have given up. This creates a stuck feeling that many people in the world end up trapped in.

The solution to this is learning how to develop a better sense of self-confidence. The solution is to learn how to step back from your ideas and not judge them harshly. Instead of shooting something down automatically, try looking at it as if a friend had asked you what you think. We change the way we perceive things when other people ask us our opinions. Self-judgment is a dangerous foe when it comes to coming up with new ideas and if we aren't confident in ourselves then we might judge far too harshly.

Developing self-confidence takes time, but it really just relies on you making the conscious decision to be kinder to yourself and to stop automatically batting down your ideas. Instead of immediately discounting what you have to say or think, try running it by someone else. Make a list of the pros and cons. Don't kill your ideas as soon as you have them, that will only lead you to ruin. I would wager that a great many people who feel like they can't ever think of any good ideas actually have plenty of good ones, they just don't have the confidence to follow after their ideas. Don't fall into a trap of discounting your ideas before you try them out. Let the world test and destroy your ideas, don't kill them yourself!

Inspiration Killer Two: Fear of Failure

Failure is one of the most misunderstood things in the world today. There are a great many people who have an intrinsic fear of failure because they think it is the worst thing that can happen to them. That fear holds them back and actively strangles any kind of creativity or innovation that individual can have. Failure, to many people seems scarier than anything else. If you fear failure, then how can you ever give yourself freedom to learn from your actions?

To be honest, there are no shortage of good ideas in the world. Even if you're struggling to figure out how to implement something or if you desire more creativity, the act of getting good ideas isn't the hardest part of being innovative. The hardest part of innovation is implementation. The art and act of implementing your ideas, taking action with your plan can cause the stomach to tighten in fear. For most people, failure is even worse than not doing anything. So, that's exactly what happens! They are so afraid they don't commit to doing something and then they bemoan their lives as not having the ideas they deeply desire.

If your fear of failure is on a subconscious level, then it's even worse. You might try as hard as you can to come up with genius ideas, but your innate fear will filter through all of them.

You might not think you have great ideas because you are too afraid to actually try and implement them.

Where does fear of failure come from? It usually comes from living in a world where failure is punished instead of praised. When a child blows it on his report card, he is berated and shamed instead of shown the power of learning from his failures. When a businessman fails at his work, he is fired or threatened instead of shown his mistakes. We live in a world where success is praised but any failure is quickly condemned. Then we act surprised when we have a world full of people who are too afraid to try anything new. The truth of the matter is that our failures will lead us to massive success in our lives because we have the opportunity to learn from them. But if our perspective about failure always remains one of fear and avoidance, then we are denying an essential part of being human.

We, as people, are always going to blow it somehow. There are some days where we are just going to completely mess everything up and there are times when an endeavor fails miserably. But if we reframed our perspective to look at these things not as bad and scary events but rather look at them as good and necessary things to happen in our lives, then we are putting ourselves in a position to grow from them. A mistake is an opportunity to learn from yourself. When you blow it, you have the opportunity to sit back, take a look at things and really ask yourself why did it happen? You have the ample opportunity to really learn from your mistakes and then learn how to avoid them in the future. This is a tremendous tool.

Those who are most successful in the world have positioned themselves to fail plenty of times. They have failed time and time again, but they never gave up. And since they never gave up, since they never let go of the thing that is most valuable to them, their desire to continue moving forward, they grew because of their failures. In a society where success is praised more than failure, we have gotten it completely backwards. Success happens only because of failure. Success is not a lack of failure; success is a sufficient amount of failures leading to growth. There are no great figures from history who haven't failed. But we don't really get to hear about their failures. We only hear about their heroic deeds and incredible actions. Politicians hide their failures from us, parents refuse to admit they failed and even the smallest hint of someone failing creates anxiety in us.

If you want to be truly innovative, if you want to create amazing ideas that will change the world then you must be willing to fail. Not only must you be willing, you must be expectant of it. Yet if you fear failure, then you will never engage in the arena of success. In order to become successful, you must fail, and that's perfectly okay! Don't fall into the trap thinking that failure is the worst thing that can happen, because it's really not. The worst thing that can happen is you making decisions out of fear, the worst that can happen is you running from your great ideas just because you are afraid of blowing it completely. Give yourself permission to screw up and then screw up! You'll learn more from a thousand failures than you will from one success.

Inspiration Killer Three: Daydreaming

Daydreaming has a serious value to creating awesome ideas and coming up with brilliant schemes and plans. But there is also a danger when you rely solely on daydreaming to create ideas. As discussed earlier, there really isn't a lack of great ideas in this world and you probably have had your fair share of awesome ideas. The problem happens when a person becomes too obsessed with thinking about their ideas instead of working to implement them.

There is a necessary amount of daydreaming required to develop an innovative idea, but it doesn't stop there. One of the greatest things that can kill inspiration is letting it sit too long in your head. Eventually it'll start to rot away. Furthermore, daydreaming and fantasy can actually harm your goals to implement your idea. Why? Because the human brain often has trouble distinguishing reality from fantasy. When you think about how great it will be to complete the big project, to finish something that you have started, the brain begins to actually think that it has done so. So, it rewards itself with dopamine, a chemical that is pleasurable, despite the fact that you haven't actually gotten started yet. This reward system for something that you failed to actually do can sabotage you in the long run because with the feelings of accomplishment stemming from daydreaming, you might find your motivation is seriously reduced. This can quickly kill your ambitions and inspiration because you are constantly in a state of *feeling* like you have already done something.

So, if you are finding that you can't really motivate yourself to work, but you have no trouble when it comes to fantasizing and daydreaming about your future, then that very could be the reason that you have no motivation. The way your brain works, it already thinks that it has done what you are fantasizing about, so it has no reason to provide you with additional motivation.

So, if that's the problem, what should you do? Get to work! Really! The time for fantasy and daydreaming is valuable in the beginning stages of a project, but if you aren't willing to get to work right away then you will be killing the valuable dreams that you have in your head. Inspiration does have an expiration date, if it stays in your head for too long it might never really see the light of day. So, when you have a good idea, when you feel that inspiration come in or if you desire to come up with some clever way to do something, just start working as soon as possible. This will change the signals in your brain away from fantasizing about the future and instead help you focus on the present, the place where the real work needs to get done!

Inspiration Killer Four: Negative People

There is nothing worse than someone who is trying to rain on your parade. The unfortunate truth of life is that we live in a world with negative, selfish people and some of these people might even try to derail your goals and desires. They might mock you and make fun of you. You might tell them your idea and they'll be the first person to shoot it down or to tell you why it won't work. And they aren't coming from a place of encouragement or compassion either. There is tremendous value in talking to someone about a problem that you see with their work, or with helpfully criticizing something, but that's not what I'm talking about. I'm talking about the people who are extremely critical because they have some kind of chip on their shoulder. These people will hurt your ambitions and can destroy your ideas if you aren't careful.

Why are these people so negative? It's usually a combination of them having bitterness toward their own failures and frustrations at the thing that they don't feel other people should be able to do. Their mindset is one of "well if I can't, then no one should!" This toxic mindset can grow within a person time after time and eventually lead to an individual completely disregarding other people's dreams. Then as you try to share your ideas with excitement, they'll proceed to try and take all of the steam and confidence out of you.

Negative people need to be removed from your life as soon as possible. You don't have any obligation to stick around these kinds of folk and there is no law requiring you to share your dreams or ambitions with these people. You have the freedom to walk away from relationships that are hurting you and destroying your inspiration. Don't fall into the trap of thinking that just because you were friends with them for a certain amount of years or that because they are your family members that you have to put up with them. Obligation is the enemy here. These toxic people use certain kinds of obligations to try and trap you into tolerating their sabotaging and painful behavior. Don't let yourself fall prey to people who have nothing better to do than to crush other people's dreams. You are much better than that! Your work is valuable, just as valuable as you are and if these toxic individuals cannot see you for that then you are far better off with making the decision to walk away. They might hate you for it, but it's better to lead someone in their own misery than to get dragged into the mud with them too.

Inspiration Killer Five: boredom

There might come a time when you feel like you aren't terribly interested in the work that you are doing. You might feel that it is a waste of time, you might feel bored or you might even feel like quitting what you are doing and electing to do something else. This is one of the most powerful killers of inspiration out there! If you become bored with your work you will stop looking at everything with curiosity, you'll stop trying to gain perspective. You'll just start watching the clock instead. You might just end up working on the project haphazardly and your work will be less than satisfactory. Your ideas will go down the drain because you aren't interested anymore.

Boredom is the danger zone to creativity. When you are bored with what you are doing then you won't have the full attentiveness, excitement or spark necessary to get things going. So, if you are in a position where you find yourself bored, what is there to do? Well, if it's a project that you are normally pretty enthusiastic about, you might just be burnt out a little bit. It would be in your best interest to take a break from your work and get some rest. Maybe direct some attention to a different subject matter entirely or just take a few days off. Boredom can seriously destroy any progress that you have made with cultivating that sense of inspiration, so don't treat it like some little thing. When you discover that you are really, deeply bored with what you are doing, you've got to do something.

If taking a break isn't an option, then you might want to consider finding things that will help you feel less bored with what you're doing. Sometimes the feeling of boredom can actually be a defense mechanism, protecting you from discomfort. If you feel bored you might actually be worried, nervous or anxious, but the boredom is masking those feelings. This can happen quite a lot, especially in an office environment. Consider asking yourself why are you bored, what could make it more fun and how can you overcome this hurdle. It's your job to make your work enjoyable, so if you are in a position to where you aren't really enjoying it, then you've got to be the one to figure out how to make it better. Don't fall into the trap of just being bored with your work and allowing that to become an excuse to slack off. You are responsible for your own interest level, so figure a way to make it fun. You could turn it into a competition, you could change up where you work, you could focus on doing a part of the job that you find more interesting first or you could spend some time daydreaming about success as a way to help motivate you to get to work. You don't get to opt out because you aren't feeling up to it!

Inspiration Killer Six: Irregularity

Inspiration finds those who are most industrious with their work. Someone who is constantly putting in hour after hour, day after day, month after month will find themselves with considerably more inspiration than someone who doesn't really bother to work every day. So, the truth is that if you aren't consistent in seeking out ideas, if you don't carve time out of your schedule to regularly try and figure out new things, you won't really have a chance. Don't let your schedule become too packed with busyness, so much so that it prevents you from getting stuff done. You must make a point to regularly work on your projects or the inspiration will never really come through.

Jerry Seinfeld talks about a productivity method known as the "Don't break the chain" system. Basically, every day that he sat down to write he would mark his calendar with a big red X. He would see how many days he could write in a row, making sure to never break the chain of X's that he would write on his calendar. If you were to adopt a system like that, to never break the chain, even if it's a little bit each day, you would find there is much more inspiration to be had in your life! Don't break the chain, instead work every possible day on what you want to do! Then you will find you have more inspiration than if you were to only work occasionally. The brain likes patterns and schedules, the more time you spend getting into a regular rhythm the quicker your brain will be able to establish the habit of finding inspiration.

Inspiration Killer Seven: Stress

Stress can be a deadly thing to our bodies! Too much stress over time and it has an adverse effect on our sleep patterns, mental health and even our blood pressure! Stress can also kill your inspiration and creativity if you aren't careful to manage it! Creativity needs a certain amount of playfulness and relaxation to be able to have room for experimentation. When you are too stressed out, the creative channels inside of you tend to shut down and your thought patterns can become too overwhelmed and negative. This makes becoming creative much harder when you feel too choked up with all of the negative things that are in your life.

So, if you want to learn to be more creative and have great ideas then you are going to need to be willing to manage your own stress levels. The more stressed out you become, the harder it is to get stuff done. So, if you haven't taken steps to learn how to decrease stress levels in your life, you really should. Not only is it healthy for your body, it's also extremely healthy for your inspiration if you were to make a conscious effort to improve your stress level.

How do we reduce our stress levels? Well everyone is different but there are a couple of things you can do to help reduce the negative stress in your life. Meditation is a great way to learn how to relax a little bit more. Breathing exercises, learning to empty your mind and sitting in quietness will allow for you to learn how to regulate your own emotions and reduce the overall stress in your life. Another great way to reduce stress is through physical exercise. The more you train your body, the harder you work out, the more your body will produce chemicals that reduce your stress. This will lower your overall stress levels and also provide you with a greater amount of energy in your daily life.

Another excellent way to deal with stress is to take some time off, get away and go on a vacation. If you aren't in a position to be able to take some time off, try finding something that you enjoy and getting involved in that. You don't always have to be working as hard as you can. Sometimes you're allowed to take a break and kick back. A lot of stress can be unnecessarily shoved on us by ourselves. Sometimes we can take too much on our plates or we might be fostering an unnecessary sense of guilt upon ourselves. It can be good and healthy for your inspiration level to be willing to step back, take a deep breath and get some rest. Don't look at resting as being lazy, look at resting as preparing yourself for the future.

Well those are all the heavy hitters when it comes to the things that can effectively kill our inspiration. If you learn to avoid and overcome these situations, you will definitely be in a much better place to overcome your own struggles and become the powerhouse of inspiration that you've always wanted to be. Before we close out this book, we're going to go ahead and look at all of the steps when it comes to generating great ideas!

Chapter 4: The Idea Generation Process

If you want to generate incredible ideas, if you want to use all of that inspiration that you've been learning to build up, then you've got to have a process! There are hundreds of different processes involved in the idea creation world, so don't feel like you are restricted to what we are about to present. Everyone is different and everyone has a different process when it comes to inventing and implementing those ideas, so if you want to add steps or remove steps, feel perfectly fine! We're going to go ahead and list out all of the steps involved in the idea generation process! Ready?

Step One: Ask Questions

The first step in coming up with a great new idea is learning to ask yourself questions. If you're trying to come up with a new idea, if you're looking for a solution, if you want to change the world around you then you are going to have to start at a questioning level. Explore as much as you can. Ask a list of questions. If you want to make a new product, ask what people need. If you want to write a book, ask yourself how can you do it differently from the world out there? The process of coming up with a brilliant new idea starts with the very concept of a question. The more questions that you can come up with, the better! Don't focus on answering those questions just yet, just ask them! Write them out and look at what you have! Several different questions you can ask include:

Why is it done that way?
- Is there a better way to do this?
- What makes this interesting to people?
- Who came up with this plan?

- What's the best way to do this?
- What's easiest?
- What's faster?
- Why is it here?
- Is it necessary?

These questions will allow you to rapidly discover information about the subject matter. If you're trying to develop a product or solve a need, you're actually really just trying to answer a question. Most people, when it comes to buying something, ask themselves "why do I need this?" It's your job to answer that question, but it starts with being able to ask the question first!

Step Two: Answer the Questions

After you've sufficiently asked the questions, after you've listed them all out, you need to then answer the questions that you have written out. You might find that there aren't sufficient answers, but that's the best part! If you can't sufficiently answer why or how then there's probably a better way to do it! This is where the very act of creating an innovative idea comes from! Good ideas are solutions to problems, so if you find a problem then you are doing a great job! Find as many problems as you can and then list them out. The answering process is all about finding a specific type of problem. For example, if you cannot answer the question of "why do most people lose their keys?" then you will be forced to research into that question. This then opens up the stage for step three!

Step Three: Research the Problems

Once you've identified certain patterns of thought that can't readily be answered, you're going to need to do some research to have a better understanding of it. For example, if you are trying to find out why most people lose their keys, you might read a few studies and learn that most people lose their keys because they are absent minded. This research gives you opportunity, if you so want it, to explore how to solve that problem. Remember the whole point of innovation and creating ideas is actually just learning how to solve problems, so when you find a problem and have sufficiently researched it, you're then going to need to brainstorm how to actually solve that problem.

Step Four: Brainstorm possible Solutions

This will be a much bigger step than the other ones but it basically involves you looking into how to solve the problem. This is where the ideas are going to come flowing and you're going to need to be able to sufficiently navigate through each idea. Remember, there are no shortage of good ideas when it comes to the human mind, the bigger problem is learning how to sift through all of them and find the best one. As you begin to figure out possible solutions, as you begin brainstorming, just write down all of the ideas that come to mind. Think hard and long about all of the different ways that you can solve this problem. As you develop more and more ideas you will find that some aren't practical and some might be impossible, but don't worry about that yet. Just write them all down. Make a point to write as many ideas as you possibly can. Don't worry about what can or cannot be done yet!

Step Five: Sift Through the Solutions

Once you've gotten a big pile of solutions, it's now time for you to make the conscious choice to start sifting through all of them. There are going to be solutions that seem doable at first but turn out to be bad ideas later on, there will be ideas that just won't work and there will be ideas that will work great after some tweaking. Your whole goal during this sifting process is to make judgment calls on each of the ideas and their merits. So, if you're looking at six possible solutions that you've come up with, you're going to need to determine how viable all of these solutions are. Some might not be, this is the appropriate stage to draw a line through them and focus on other things. If you've done it right, you should have been able to determine which solutions will actually work and which ones won't. Then you're going to need to proceed to the next step.

Step Six: Pick One

The man who chases after everything will gain nothing. Don't try to fit all of those solutions into one big package, instead just pick one and make the choice to develop that solution. This is probably the hardest part of finding solutions to problems because we often want to roll as many things as we can into one big process, but that's not the best possible idea. The best idea is to focus on only one thing at a time. When you pick your single solution, you have a better chance of learning how to implement it, figure it out and develop it than if you picked three solutions and tried to work on all three simultaneously. This is probably one of the harder aspects of coming up with a great idea because when we are faced with several good ideas it can be difficult to choose just one. We might even feel that to choose one we are calling the other solutions bad ideas. Not at all! Some solutions are great ideas but once again, there are *no shortage of good ideas in the world!* There is, however, a shortage of implementation, so if you find yourself struggling to pick between two or three solutions, just pick one. Getting it done is worth more than having a better idea!

Step Seven: Experiment

After you've figured out your solution you're going to need to spend serious time working on it until it is actually existing! Whatever the solution is, this is the part where you begin to focus on moving it from your head into reality. If you are trying to build an invention this would involve you actually making a prototype. If it's a book or play, it's going to involve you actually writing it. Implementation is an insanely integral part of being innovative, an idea formed is only one half of the equation. You must be willing to work on it and do it as well! As you're working on your new idea, you might find that you have more ideas to support them, this is a good thing! You should feel free to allow your plans and projects to expand as you work. Don't lose your focus on what you are planning on doing, but as you work feel free to add more to what you are doing.

The most important part of about this is having a freedom and playfulness to keep trying and experimenting with what you are doing. Some things might not work out, but that's okay. The more you experiment and work on it, the more you are able to develop this prototype, whatever it is, the more concrete your idea will become. If the idea ends up being a disaster, that's fine! You still have other solutions that you've developed, so all you need to do is go back and work on a different solution. Experimentation is extremely important to this process because it allows for you to figure out what works and what doesn't.

Step Eight: Finalization

The last and final step in the process is finalization. This happens after you have gone through all of the testing, planning and preparing stages. This is where you actually bring your idea into the world for people to interact with. If you are an artist, this would be when you unveil your work. If you are trying to develop a new strategy for your company this is when you would implement that new plan. This phase is the final phase of the idea process. Ideas start as mere concepts, little seeds but eventually those seeds grow enough to where they are able to actually interact with the real world. The whole point of a good idea isn't simply to feel good about what you have thought up, the whole point of a good idea is being able to share it with the world in real, tangible form. The finalization process is what brings it all together.

Conclusion:

Are you feeling inspired now? We've spent a great deal of time talking about the inspiration process. We've looked at how inspiration isn't a single event that happens to you, rather we've learned that inspiration grows in us and is dependent on our desire to cultivate a sense of growth and understanding within ourselves. We've looked at the dangers to inspiration, the deadly things that can reduce our ability to generate innovative ideas and we've learned how to overcome them. You have the greatest capacity there is to generate incredible and interesting new ideas! It might not be easy and while other people might look at the amazing ideas that are in the world and believe they exist because of some sort of magic, the truth is that these ideas come from hard work, dedication and a desire to change the world. You can generate incredible ideas, all you need is focus, effort and the desire to dream big!

Other books available by Michael Sloan on Kindle, paperback and audio:

The Art of Thinking Big: How to Establish and Reach Your Goals, Be Successful and Achieve Anything You Want In Life

The Art of Public Speaking: How to Speak In Front of an Audience without Fear

The Art of Problem Solving 101: Improve Your Critical Thinking And Decision Making Skills And Learn How To Solve Problems Creatively

Positive Thinking with Action: How to Fight Back Against Negative Thought Patterns and Win at Life

Sun Tzu & Machiavelli Success and Leadership Principles: Based On the Classics the Art of War and the Prince

The Fearless Mindset: The Empowering Secrets To Living Life Without Fear And Worry

The Art of Being Prolific: How to Be Ten Times More Productive with Your Day